September Reign

By Stephanie M. Captain

Modern Day Proverbs and Meditations

Dedication

As always, God you Rock!

Thank you for everything.

Acknowledgements

For Resheemah with Love---keep fighting the good fight of faith.

To my family: My husband Amos, children, Amos II, Ashley, Aaron & Chantel. For my grandsons Simien and Asher---I love you all so much.

To my Pastors, my mother, my sisters and brothers, God-parents, and God-children and church family---thanks for all the prayers and support.

Pastor Pam your encouragement and investments in me will pay off, soon.

No prayer life is equivalent to
having a blind person drive you around.

Tenacity is like CPR to your dreams.

Know who you are,

Or the devil

Will find a role for you to play.

Too many people walk around with

Spiritual handicap stickers because

It's just easier

For someone else to carry them.

Sometimes it is not about what you
Confide in your best friend,

But the freedom experienced just
Because you had a platform to vent.

Play out

Your daily schedule

In prayer each morning.

That will eliminate all pressure,
Because by the time it happens,

It is just a rerun.

When our faith

Mixes with His Word on healing,

We will have children call health.

When up are up against back stabbers,

Just turn around and let them come

Face to face with the God in you.

We all have an expiration date.

Your job is making sure the right Kingdom gets your remains.

When your dreams don't make sense

Open your eyes

And see what God sees for you.

If you are going to bring me a bone,

At least let me

Pick the meat I want off of it;

Otherwise, just bury it.

Before you start a war

You must conquer

The enemy within you first.

Sometimes your toughest situations can be resolved by the ABCs

Accept God can handle it

Believe you will make it

Carry on in the meantime

Waiting doesn't equate sitting,

It means working until you meet your
desires somewhere along the way.

You may be fooled by some things a person says,

But fruit does not lie.

Sometimes you just have to come to
terms with some things and admit

That you really haven't truly

Put it all in God's hands,

And there is a grave possibility

You never will.

Lies have many different faces.

You can't catch the wind,

But you can allow it to carry you.

The heart can be deceitful

The mind can lie

The tongue can convince

But all of them bow to Him.

When people are so eager to convince
others of the flaws in your character,

That is a good sign that you are well on
your way;

I call it fanfare.

What you say and what you see will never add up until you add faith with it.

Loving God should have nothing to do
with what He is doing for you,

But everything to do with

What He's done already.

Love is not a whimsical fairy tale,

It is the warrior

That gets in the trenches; to defend and
Protect what it knows belongs to it.

Creating another Way

Will not

Get you to the same destination,

Just a wider road to sorrow.

Fear and Faith have never been friends,

Although they often live

Right next door to each other.

Mercy always comes at a price

Few are willing to pay.

Beauty is not always

In the eye of the beholder

But rest in the wisdom of the Creator.

Mocking is a cruel enemy

That often sits at the dinner table.

Getting it together doesn't mean

You will be perfect,

Just held together enough

To start moving again.

Windows can serve

As a prison or an escape route.

It depends on whether

You look up or down.

It is ridiculous to argue with a mind
that is already determined to fail.

My legs will always be taking me to
something or away from something,

I can tell which one

By the speed in which I am walking.

Can't is not a dirty word

Just often misplaced

I can't fail

I can't lose

I can't stay where there is negativity.

Many times it is not

Encouragement you need,

Just a good song

To jumpstart the rhythm

You've been given by the Creator.

The difference in a

Massage

and a

Message

Is often the one giving it.

Thoughts can either

Liberate you or imprison you.

The past will often greet you

So you must remove the welcome mat,

Before its arrival.

It is the power of the One listening to the prayers that get you the results.

Right is not always an action,

But a position

That forces your decisions

To line up with it.

Humility has few comrades,

Yet it outranks and out lasts chief enemies.

The trick with God fighting your battles

Is allowing Him to do it

Without you throwing illegal punches

That will disqualify you every time.

Faith will always be tested.

The important thing to remember

Is that it is not a remedial test,

But a post test that determines your
next level of advancement.

If someone else's praise

Is louder than yours

Don't be concerned,

Their battle may be bigger.

You will know you have matured

When your concern

Is not just for your cabin,

But the entire ship.

What the head does

Affects the tail,

So if you are running around in circles…

If you tangle your self-esteem

With that of others

You are bound to choke the life from
yourself and them.

Fruition is a harvest

That doesn't come cheap.

When you find yourself

On the outskirts,

Just thank God

For new land development

And put up a city limits sign.

Complaining is like sucking in helium

And then trying to have a conversation.

Just doesn't sound right,

And it is hard to take you seriously.

Hatred knows many people,

But doesn't get along with any of them.

Most people

Will still form an opinion despite what

Truth whispers

Or good people yell.

The best way to move on,

Is to move on.

Some people's promises

Are no valuable

Than the prize in the cereal box.

When you learn to live to impact

Rather than impress

Mountains

Suddenly become level plains.

If you learn to choose your battles

You won't always be winded.

Backsliding is like playing

Russian roulette

With all the chambers filled.

Having Godly character means

Your reputation arrives

Long before you do

And lingers long after you are gone.

To cease being critical is like

Giving a blind man his sight back.

There is nothing

You can or cannot do

To eliminate being

The subject of discussion,

So just make sure you give the talkers
Good listening materials.

All too often you will find yourself in
Relationships you didn't know you had

Because of what you believed you have
Shared with people

You thought you could trust.

It is not that faith

Does not see what is going on,

It just chooses to see

Beyond what it sees.

Sick by symptoms

Healed by confession.

In many cases it will be the mind

That is released from its life sentence

Before

Any prison doors are ever opened.

Indeed there are many paths,

Yet still one Door.

You are either acting out

Where you've been

Or foreshadowing

Where you are going;

Either way,

Your story is being told.

The things that impact life the greatest

Usually begin

With the smallest choices.

You may not be able to lead a person
Where you have not been,

But God whispering the directions in
Your ears will get you both there.

I smile,

Not because of where I am sometimes,

But because

Of where He has told me I am going.

When you get your stuff

And you are so overjoyed

That you no longer

Remember who gave it to you,

Your message is clear;

It really wasn't

The giver you were after.

Kindness is 3 fold

What I refuse to say

What I refuse to do

What I refuse to believe.

You must be as interested in drama

As you would be

In getting a bad case of hives.

Love is the only thing I know that can

Cover dirt and remain clean

Hear trash

And not become contaminated

Live on the mountain

And the valley at the same time.

Hope and faith

Are the cheerleaders

That see the final score

Before the clock ever starts.

Sidelines were never made for the
People running in the race.

My faith is not based

On what I see

But what I believe.

It doesn't matter how many other
People believe in you,

You must be one of them.

If you are bold enough

To throw a rock and hide your hand,

Don't act surprised

When you get hit in the head with one.

Man may not always

Give you the credit,

But God

Will never confuse your deposits.

What doesn't come out in the wash

Will most assuredly be

Consumed by the heat of the dryer.

Your willingness to wait

For clear instructions

Is an indication

Of how important

The dispatcher is to you.

Sometimes

Healing is a process

In which

Many deaths take place

Before it comes to maturity.

Jesus hears the quietest of whispers.

Forgiveness is my epipen.

You know when you have truly forgiven someone when you no longer wish them any harm. When you have left their judgment up to God. When you can wish them well, and no longer trouble yourself with their fate.